P9-CSW-784

I made this
book for:

_____

Love,

Alona

Once Upon a Potty

boy

Once Upon

boy

FIREFLY BOOKS

a Potty

Written and illustrated by Alona Frankel

A Firefly Book

Published by Firefly Books Ltd. 2007

Text and Illustrations Copyright © 2007 Alona Frankel

All rights reserved. No part of this publication may be reproduced, stored in a retrieval system, or transmitted in any form or by any means, electronic, mechanical, photocopying, recording or otherwise, without the prior written permission of the Publisher.

Seventh printing, 2013

Publisher Cataloging-in-Publication Data (U.S.)
Frankel, Alona.
    Once upon a potty : boy / Alona Frankel.
Originally published: Hauppauge, NY : Barron's
Educational Series, 1980.
[40] p. : col. ill. ; cm.
Summary: Explains in simple text and illustrations why and how a little boy uses a potty.
ISBN-13: 978-1-55407-283-5
ISBN-10: 1-55407-283-2
1. Toilet training -- Juvenile literature. 2. Boys -- Health and hygiene – Juvenile literature. I. Title.
649.62 dc22   HQ770.5.F718   2007

Library and Archives Canada
Cataloguing in Publication
Frankel, Alona
    Once upon a potty : boy / written and illustrated by Alona Frankel.
ISBN-13: 978-1-55407-283-5
ISBN-10: 1-55407-283-2
1. Toilet training--Juvenile literature. 2. Boys--Health and hygiene--Juvenile literature. I. Title.
HQ770.5.F73 2007   j649'.62   C2006-906724-4

Published in the United States by
Firefly Books (U.S.) Inc.
P.O. Box 1338, Ellicott Station
Buffalo, New York 14205

Published in Canada by
Firefly Books Ltd.
50 Staples Avenue, Unit #1
Richmond Hill, Ontario, Canada L4B 0A7

The publisher gratefully acknowledges the financial support for our publishing program by the Government of Canada through the Book Publishing Industry Development Program.

"Once Upon a Potty," "Joshua" and "Prudence" are registered trademarks of Alona Frankel •
www.alonafrankel.com

All "Once Upon a Potty" properties are administered exclusively by Child Matters Corporation •
www.infochild.com

Manufactured by Printplus Limited in Shen Zhen, Guang Dong, P.R.China in September, 2013, Job #S130900075.

Printed in China

To my sons, Ari and Michael

Motto:

Panta Rei
(Everything Flows)

– *Heracleitus*

Dear Fellow-Parents,

Once Upon a Potty is best used as a companion volume to a child's new potty. I wrote this book when my own child was toilet training to help him better understand the process. My son was encouraged and excited by this story. It motivated him to make the developmental leap from diaper to potty.

Potty talk has long been considered taboo in conversation – even between parent and child. Thankfully, this attitude is changing, and children and parents are all the happier for it. I believe that a frank and open approach to all bodily functions is a good, healthy attitude toward child rearing. I have decided to use "Wee-Wee" and "Poo-Poo" in this book, but I encourage you to read the story with your child using words most suitable for you and your family.

Learning to use the potty is often a lengthy process, taxing the patience of both parent and child. When success finally comes – and it should come in its own good time without undue pressure or haste – it enhances the child's confidence and pride. He has taken another step toward independence. He sat on the potty as a little child and got up feeling ten feet tall.

It's one small step for mankind, but a giant one for your family.

Love,

Alona

Hello. I am Joshua's mother.
I'd like to tell you about Joshua
and his new potty.

This is Joshua.
Joshua is a little boy.

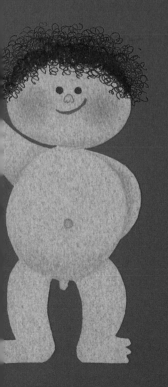

Just like you, Joshua has a body,
and this body has many nice and useful parts:

A head for thinking

Eyes for seeing

Ears for hearing

A mouth to talk
and eat with

Hands for playing

A pee-pee for
making
Wee-Wee

Legs for walking
and running

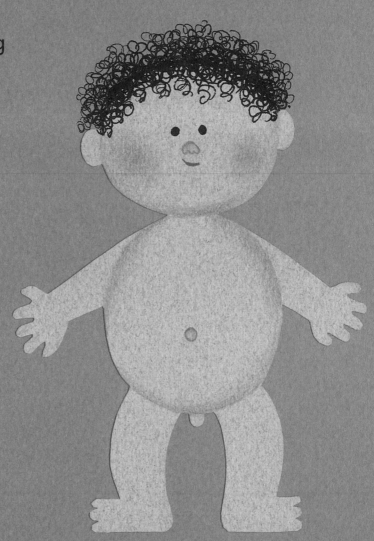

A bottom for sitting
and in it a little hole
for making Poo-Poo.

Ever since Joshua was born, he has been making
Wee-Wee and Poo-Poo into his diaper, and I,
his mother, have been changing him.
He was doing it when he was two days old.

He was doing it when he was two months old.

And here you see him,
still doing it,
and me, his mother,
changing him.

A clean diaper

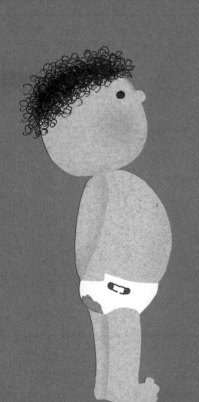

A diaper with
Wee-Wee and
Poo-Poo

A diaper with
Wee-Wee and
Poo-Poo

A clean
diaper

Until, one day, Joshua's grandmother
bought him a big present.

Joshua opened the box and found
a strange something inside.

Was it a hat?
No, it wasn't a hat.

Was it a milk bowl for the cat?
No, it wasn't a milk bowl
for the cat.

Was it a flowerpot?
No, it wasn't a flowerpot.

Was it a birdbath?
No, it wasn't a birdbath.

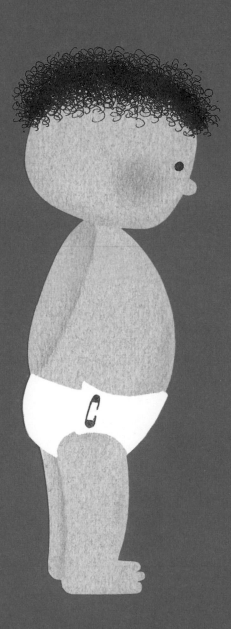

It was a potty, for sitting on and making
Wee-Wee and Poo-Poo into, instead of a diaper.
How wonderful!
Joshua was very happy.

He sat on his new potty
and sat and sat and sat and sat
and nothing came out,
neither Wee-Wee nor Poo-Poo.

Later on he made
both Wee-Wee and Poo-Poo,
but not EXACTLY into the potty.

Afterwards he kept making Wee-Wee
and Poo-Poo into his diaper and I,
Joshua's mother, kept changing him.

Until, one day, when Joshua had a feeling
that Poo-Poo was ready to come out,
he ran to his potty and sat down on it.

He sat
and sat and sat and sat and sat
and sat and sat and sat and sat
and sat and sat and sat and sat
and sat and sat and sat and sat
and sat and sat and sat and sat
and sat and sat and sat and sat
and sat and sat and sat and sat
and sat and sat and sat and sat
and sat and sat and sat and sat
and sat and sat and sat and sat
and sat and sat and sat and sat
and sat and sat and sat and sat
and sat and sat and sat and sat
and sat and sat and sat and sat
and sat and sat and sat and sat
and sat and sat and sat and sat
and sat and sat and sat and sat
and sat and sat and sat and sat
and sat and sat and sat and sat

and when he got up and looked into his potty
he saw all of his Wee-Wee and Poo-Poo
RIGHT INSIDE IT!

Joshua was very happy and proud and came to show me his full potty and I, Joshua's mother, was also very happy, and proud of Joshua.

And then the two of us,
I, Joshua's mother, and Joshua,
carried the potty to the bathroom
and emptied it into the toilet.

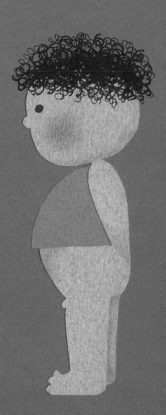

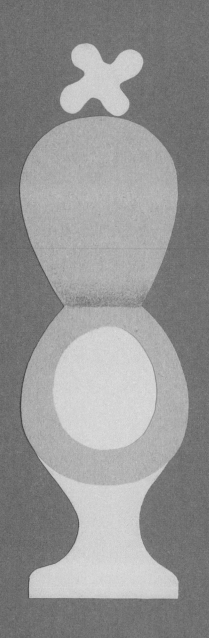

"Bye-bye, Wee-Wee.
Bye-bye, Poo-Poo,"
said Joshua, and then
washed his hands.

And now he likes
his potty even more
and uses it every time.

Alona Frankel is
the author and illustrator
of over thirty titles for children.
She is the recipient of numerous
awards, and her books and art
are seen all around the world.
Ms. Frankel lives in
Tel Aviv, Israel.

To find out more
about Alona, visit
www.alonafrankel.com